# INCLUSIVE MEDIA PLANNING

## A GUIDE TO CRAFTING INCLUSIVE CAMPAIGNS

CHRISTOPHER HOLMES

# CONTENTS

CHAPTER ONE

# DIVERSITY, EQUALITY AND INCLUSION
# IN MEDIA PLANNING

Diversity, equality, and inclusion (DEI) are interconnected principles that are becoming more essential in many aspects of society, including media planning. In basic words, diversity refers to the representation of a range of viewpoints, experiences, and backgrounds in a particular space. Equity relates to fairness and justice in the allocation of resources and opportunities, whereas inclusion is about building a friendly and supportive atmosphere where everyone feels valued and respected.

Being truly inclusive on social media means finding ways to make the content both physically accessible and visibly diverse. Everyone wants access to content, they want to see themselves represented in it

When it comes to media planning, DEI is about ensuring that all groups are correctly and respectfully portrayed in the media and that media planning choices take into consideration the opinions and experiences of various populations. This involves assessing the demographic composition of the target audience and the cultural environment in which the media will be consumed, as well as the influence that media may have on changing society's attitudes and conventions.

Media has a crucial influence in moulding public opinion

and views, and media planning choices must reflect the variety of people. For example, if a media campaign is geared toward a largely Hispanic audience, it's necessary to analyze the cultural allusions and values that connect with this group and to ensure that the language used is suitable and culturally relevant.

In addition, media planning choices must be fair, which involves evaluating the influence that media might have on underrepresented populations. This involves being cognizant of how media may promote negative stereotypes and prejudice, and actively striving to prevent these impacts by considering various viewpoints and experiences in media planning choices.

Finally, inclusion is about establishing an atmosphere where everyone feels appreciated and respected, regardless of their origin or identity. This involves understanding the value of representation and making sure that different populations are involved and represented in media planning choices. This involves evaluating the effect that media may have on those who are generally marginalized or underrepresented, such as persons with disabilities, members of the LGBTQ+ community, and other minority groups.

.

Diversity, equality, and inclusion are key components of good media strategy. By ensuring that media planning choices appropriately represent people and are fair and inclusive, media planners may assist to promote good social change and develop a more just and inclusive society.

# CHAPTER TWO

## OVERCOMING UNCONSCIOUS BIAS
## IN MEDIA PLANNING

Unconscious bias refers to the attitudes and opinions that we have subconsciously and which might impact our judgments and behaviours. In media planning, unconscious bias may have a substantial influence on the representation of various groups in the media and the messages that are transmitted. This might encompass anything from the selection of pictures, and the language used in commercials, to the media platforms that are used to target diverse demographics.

Unconscious prejudice may result in a lack of representation or stereotyped depiction of particular groups, which can promote negative stereotypes and discrimination. For example, research has found that women are generally underrepresented in commercials, and when they are included, they are often shown in conventional positions, such as homemakers or beauty product consumers. Additionally, people of colour are frequently represented in stereotyped ways, such as being shown as criminals or being depicted in a manner that perpetuates negative assumptions about their culture.

To avoid unconscious bias in media planning, it's vital to be aware of its influence and to actively try to overcome it. Here are a few techniques to combat unconscious bias in media planning:

Conduct a biased audit: A bias audit entails assessing your existing media planning methods and finding places where unconscious prejudice may be present. This might allow you to identify how unconscious bias is impacting your media planning choices and to build measures to remedy it.

Diversify your team: Having a broad team of individuals with varied experiences and opinions participating in media planning may assist to avoid unconscious bias. This is because individuals from diverse backgrounds may have varied viewpoints and experiences that may guide media planning choices and assist to identify places where unconscious prejudice may be prevalent.

Use inclusive language: The language used in media planning may have a big influence on how diverse groups are depicted. To overcome unconscious prejudice, it's crucial to adopt language that is inclusive and courteous and to avoid terminology that is stereotyped or insulting.

Consider the cultural context: When creating media campaigns, it's crucial to consider the cultural environment in which the media will be received. This entails knowing the views, beliefs, and experiences of the target audience and ensuring that the media represents these viewpoints.

Seek input from various groups: Engaging with various groups and soliciting their opinion on media planning choices might assist to overcome unconscious prejudice. This is because individuals from diverse backgrounds may have varied viewpoints and experiences that may assist to identify places where unconscious bias may be prevalent and affect media planning choices.

In conclusion, unconscious bias can have a significant impact on media planning, leading to a lack of representation or stereotypical representation of certain groups. To counteract unconscious bias, it's important to be aware of its impact and to actively work to address it, such as by conducting a biased audit, diversifying your team, using inclusive language, considering cultural context, and seeking feedback from diverse groups. By addressing unconscious bias in media planning, we can help to promote positive social change and foster a more just and inclusive society

# CHAPTER THREE

## CONSIDERING INTERSECTIONALITY IN MEDIA PLANNING

Intersectionality is a concept that acknowledges the interaction of diverse types of oppression and privilege depending on criteria such as race, gender, sexual orientation, and socio-economic background. In media planning, understanding intersectionality is crucial because it helps to ensure that media campaigns authentically represent the experiences and opinions of various populations and are inclusive and egalitarian.

For example, while creating a media campaign geared at a Black, female audience, intersectionality would necessitate analyzing the experiences and opinions of this audience in terms of both their race and gender. This can entail assessing the influence that media can have on propagating negative stereotypes about Black women and actively striving to avoid these impacts by integrating different viewpoints and experiences in media planning choices.

Another example is addressing the intersectionality of the LGBTQ+ community, which comprises a varied variety of experiences and identities depending on criteria such as sexual orientation, gender identity, and race. In media planning, it's crucial to examine the experiences and viewpoints of the LGBTQ+ community and to ensure that media campaigns appropriately represent this variety. This might involve utilizing inclusive language, eliminating damaging stereotypes, and ensuring that the media is reflective of the LGBTQ+ community in terms of its experiences and opinions.

In addition to addressing intersectionality in terms of the intended audience, it's also crucial to evaluate the influence that media might have on the larger society. For example, media may have a considerable influence on establishing society's attitudes and norms, and it's crucial to analyze how media might perpetuate or counteract negative stereotypes and prejudice based on intersecting identities.

To guarantee that media planning choices include intersectionality, it's necessary to have a diverse team of individuals with varied experiences and viewpoints working in media planning. This may assist to identify areas where intersectionality may be significant and ensure that media planning choices are inclusive and equitable.

Incorporating intersectionality in media planning is vital because it helps to guarantee that media campaigns appropriately represent the experiences and viewpoints of various populations and are inclusive and equitable. By examining the interaction of diverse types of oppression and privilege, media planners may assist to promote good social change and develop a more fair and inclusive society.

CHAPTER FOUR

# REACHING AND ENGAGING UNDERREPRESENTED GROUPS IN MEDIA PLANNING

R eaching and involving marginalized groups in media planning is vital to ensure that media efforts are inclusive and fair. Here are some excellent practices for reaching and engaging underrepresented populations in media planning:

Conduct research: Understanding the experiences, attitudes, and needs of underrepresented groups is crucial to successfully reach and engereachingem. This might entail conducting focus groups, polls, and market research to get insights into these populations and their media consumption patterns.

Use varied media channels: Distinct underrepresented groups may have different media consumption patterns, and it's crucial to consider this when picking media outlets to reach them. This may involve employing a combination of conventional and digital media platforms, such as television, radio, social media, and print media.

Consider the cultural context: When organizing media campaigns, it's crucial to consider the cultural environment in which the media will be received. This entails knowing the views, beliefs, and experiences of the target audience and ensuring that the media represents these viewpoints.

Use inclusive language: The language used in media planning may have a substantial influence on how underrepresented groups are portrayed. To ensure that media efforts are inclusive and fair, it's crucial to utilize language that is polite and inclusive and to avoid terminology that is stereotyped or offensive.

Collaborate with community organizations: Partnering with community organizations that serve underrepresented groups may be an effective method to reach and engage these populations. Various organizations may give vital insights into the lives and viewpoints of these groups and can assist to ensure that media campaigns are culturally appropriate and relevant.

Measure success: It's crucial to constantly review the performance of media initiatives in reaching and engaging underrepresented populations. This might entail measuring data like reach, engagement, and conversion rates, and utilizing these indicators to influence future media planning choices.

Addressing and involving disadvantaged groups in media planning demands a sophisticated and culturally sensitive approach. By conducting research, using diverse media channels, considering cultural context, using inclusive language, collaborating with community organizations, and measuring success, media planners can help to ensure that media campaigns are inclusive and equitable and effectively reach and engage underrepresented groups.

# CHAPTER FIVE

## IMPORTANCE OF DATA AND ANALYTICS IN INCLUSIVE MEDIA PLANNING

Data and analytics play a significant role in supporting inclusive media strategy by offering insights into the behaviour and preferences of various audiences. This information may be utilized to create educated media planning choices that are more inclusive and fair. Here are some ways that data and analytics may be utilized to support inclusive media planning:

Demographic data: Understanding the demographic mix of distinct target groups is crucial to efficient media strategy. Demographic data may give insights into aspects such as age, gender, ethnicity, income, and geographic location, which can be utilized to guide media planning choices.

Media consumption data: Media consumption data gives insights into how various target audiences consume media, including the sorts of media they consume and when they consume it. This information may be utilized to make educated judgments regarding media channel selection and scheduling.

Audience insights: Data from sources like social media, search engines, and online forums may give useful insights into the attitudes, views, and preferences of distinct target groups. This information may be used to guide media planning choices, such as the sort of material to develop and the tone of the message to deploy.

Campaign performance data: Data on the success of media campaigns may be used to guide future media planning choices. This includes data on reach, engagement, conversion rates, and other analytics, which may be utilized to enhance media planning methods and increase the performance of future campaigns.

Predictive analytics: Predictive analytics may be used to find patterns and trends in data and generate predictions about future audience behaviour. This information may be used to guide media planning choices, such as targeting strategies, budget allocation, and content production.

Data and analytics play a crucial role in supporting inclusive media design by offering useful insights into the behaviour and preferences of various audiences. By utilizing data to guide media planning choices, media planners may guarantee that media campaigns are inclusive and equitable and successfully reach and engage underrepresented populations.

**Diversity in Media Ownership and Leadership**
Promoting diversity in media ownership and leadership is vital for ensuring that media authentically represents the experiences and opinions of various populations. However, there are various barriers to encouraging

diversity in media ownership and leadership, including:

Lack of representation: There is a considerable underrepresentation of women, persons of race, and other underrepresented groups in media ownership and leadership roles. This reduces the range of ideas and experiences that are portrayed in media and might lead to a homogenized media environment.

Lack of access to finance and resources: Underrepresented groups typically face challenges in obtaining capital and resources, which may hinder them from launching media firms or purchasing existing media outlets. This restricts the variety of media ownership and may lead to a lack of representation in media leadership roles.

Unconscious bias: Unconscious biases may affect decision-making in media ownership and leadership, leading to a lack of diversity in these roles. For example, unconscious biases might lead to the advancement of persons who are similar to those already in power, rather than those who contribute a broader viewpoint.

To encourage diversity in media ownership and leadership, numerous measures may be undertaken, including:

Government efforts: Governments may establish measures to encourage the growth of media firms owned by underrepresented groups. This might involve giving access to finance and resources, tax advantages, and assistance for media entrepreneurship initiatives.

Industry initiatives: The media industry can take steps

to promote diversity in media ownership and leadership by implementing diversity and inclusion programs, promoting diversity in hiring and promotion practices and providing mentorship and training opportunities for underrepresented groups.\sDiversifying investment portfolios: Investors can play a role in promoting diversity in media ownership by diversifying their investment portfolios to include media businesses owned by underrepresented groups. This may assist to give funds and resources to support the development of these enterprises.

Addressing unconscious bias: It's important to address unconscious bias in media ownership and leadership by providing training and education on the impact of unconscious bias, implementing systems to identify and mitigate bias, and creating inclusive workplace cultures that promote diversity and equity.

Fostering diversity in media ownership and leadership is vital for ensuring that media authentically represents the experiences and opinions of different populations. Addressing the difficulties of lack of representation, lack of access to money and resources, and unconscious prejudice needs a multi-faceted strategy that involves government measures, industry activities, diversifying investment portfolios, and addressing unconscious bias. By applying these ideas, media may become more inclusive and fair, appropriately portraying the experiences and opinions of various populations.

# CHAPTER SIX

## PRODUCING CULTURALLY ACCEPTABLE AND INCLUSIVE MESSAGES

Developing culturally competent and inclusive messaging is crucial for ensuring that media successfully reaches and engages various audiences. Here are some critical elements for establishing culturally competent and inclusive messaging:

Conduct research: Research to understand the cultures, attitudes, and viewpoints of the varied audiences you are addressing. This entails knowing the specific issues and experiences of diverse groups, as well as their communication preferences and practices.

Create a diversified team: Develop a diverse team to work on communications, including persons from the populations you are targeting. This may assist to ensure that the message is culturally appropriate and truthful and that it successfully connects with varied audiences.

Avoid stereotypes: Stereotypes may be damaging and encourage negative thoughts and attitudes. When developing messaging, it is important to avoid stereotypes and instead, focus on accurately representing the experiences and perspectives of diverse communities.

Use inclusive language: Inclusive language is critical for promoting equity and reducing bias. When developing messaging, it is important to use language that is inclusive, non-offensive, and sensitive to the experiences of diverse communities.

Test and refine messaging: Test messaging with diverse audiences to ensure that it resonates and is culturally sensitive. Use feedback from these tests to refine and improve messaging, making adjustments as needed to better meet the needs and preferences of diverse audiences.

Regularly evaluate and update messaging: Regularly evaluate and update messaging to ensure that it remains culturally competent and inclusive. This includes monitoring feedback from diverse audiences and making changes as needed to ensure that messaging continues to effectively reach and engage these communities.

Developing culturally competent and inclusive messaging is essential for ensuring that media effectively reaches and engages diverse audiences. By doing research, developing a diverse team, avoiding stereotypes, utilizing inclusive language, testing and refining message, and frequently assessing and updating messaging, media may generate messaging that is culturally sensitive and successful in reaching and engaging different populations.

## Cross-cultural Communication in Media Planning

Navigating the challenges of cross-cultural communication in media planning is vital for ensuring that media authentically represents the experiences and opinions of many populations and successfully reaches and engages these audiences. Here are some critical factors for negotiating cross-cultural communication in media planning:

Cultural awareness: Developing cultural awareness is vital for understanding the beliefs, values, and communication preferences of varied populations. This entails knowing the distinctive experiences and viewpoints of diverse cultures, as well as the historical and political settings in which these groups exist.

Avoid cultural appropriation: Cultural appropriation is the use of components of one culture by members of another culture without sufficient knowledge or respect for the culture being appropriated. In media planning, it is crucial to prevent cultural appropriation by authentically expressing the experiences and viewpoints of various populations and avoiding the usage of cultural features in a disrespectful or insensitive way.

Language considerations: Language is a crucial element in cross-cultural communication. When producing communications, it is crucial to consider the linguistic preferences of varied cultures and to utilize language that is culturally sensitive and inclusive. This may involve employing numerous languages to address diverse audiences, or adopting culturally appropriate vocabulary and wording.

Respect for cultural norms: Cultural norms are the common ideas, attitudes, and behaviours that are indicative of a given society. When crafting messaging, it is crucial to respect cultural norms by avoiding information that is objectionable or inconsiderate of the experiences and opinions of other populations.

Consider the cultural context: Cultural context refers to the social, historical, and political variables that affect the experiences and viewpoints of distinct cultures. When producing communications, it is crucial to incorporate cultural context by authentically expressing the experiences and opinions of varied cultures and avoiding anything that perpetuates negative stereotypes or maintains uneven power relations.

Test messaging with various audiences: Testing messaging with different audiences is vital for ensuring that the message is culturally responsive and successful in reaching and engaging these cultures. Use feedback from these tests to refine and enhance the message, making revisions as appropriate to better match the requirements and preferences of varied audiences.

Negotiating the complexity of cross-cultural communication in media planning is crucial for ensuring that media authentically represents the experiences and opinions of varied populations and successfully reaches and engages these audiences. By gaining cultural awareness, avoiding cultural appropriation, considering language, honouring cultural norms, considering cultural context, and testing messages with varied audiences, media may manage cross-cultural communication in a culturally sensitive and successful way.

## The Future of Inclusive Media Planning

The future of inclusive media planning has enormous promise for pushing progress towards more diversity, equality, and inclusion in media. Here are three major areas in which technology is positioned to accelerate success in inclusive media planning:

Data and analytics: Advances in data and analytics are helping media firms to better understand the requirements and preferences of varied audiences, as well as to measure the efficacy of their attempts to reach these audiences. With greater data and analytics, media businesses can make more educated choices about which channels and platforms to utilize for reaching and engaging diverse audiences, and can constantly refine and improve their strategies for reaching these groups.

Artificial intelligence: Artificial intelligence is altering the way media firms develop, distribute, and assess the effectiveness of their content. With AI, media businesses can automate many of the tedious and time-consuming procedures involved in media planning, freeing up more time and resources to concentrate on the creation of inclusive messages and the discovery of new possibilities to reach different audiences.

Virtual and augmented reality: Virtual and augmented

reality are creating new options for media firms to engage different audiences in engaging and immersive ways. With these tools, media businesses can develop extremely immersive content that correctly represents the experiences and opinions of varied populations and that connects with these viewers.

Social media: Social media is an increasingly crucial platform for reaching and engaging diverse audiences, providing media firms with a direct line of contact with these groups. With the continuous rise of social media, media firms have the chance to interact with diverse audiences in new and inventive ways, and to harness this medium to generate a more inclusive message that resonates with these groups.

The future of inclusive media planning has enormous promise for pushing progress towards more diversity, equality, and inclusion in media. With advances in data and analytics, AI, virtual and augmented reality, and social media, media companies have the tools they need to reach and engage diverse audiences in innovative and effective ways, and to create more inclusive messaging that accurately reflects the experiences and perspectives of these communities.

Here are some examples of effective inclusive media planning initiatives:

Procter & Gamble's "My Black is Beautiful": This program was started by Procter & Gamble in 2007 as a method to promote the beauty and variety of Black women and to address the underrepresentation of Black women in media. The campaign contained a series of advertisements showcasing actual Black women, and it was backed by a website and social media presence that gave a venue for Black women to share their experiences and interact with one another.

Coca-"Taste Cola's the Feeling": This global campaign from Coca-Cola was designed to celebrate the diversity of the brand's consumers and to reach a broader range of audiences. The campaign featured a series of ads that showcased people from different cultures, ethnicities, and backgrounds, and it was accompanied by a social media presence that encouraged consumers to share their own stories and experiences.

Disney's "#DreamBigPrincess": This initiative from Disney was designed to empower young girls and to promote positive representation of women and girls in media. The campaign featured a series of ads and videos that showcased strong, confident, and independent female characters, and it was accompanied by a social media presence that encouraged young girls to share their dreams and aspirations.

Nike's "Equality": This campaign from Nike was designed to promote diversity and inclusiveness in sports and to address the underrepresentation of women and people of colour in the world of sports. The campaign contained a series of advertisements and films that showed athletes from diverse backgrounds, and it was complemented by a social media presence that invited customers to submit their tales and experiences.

Google's "Year in Search": This yearly campaign from Google shows the most searched-for subjects of the year, and it is aimed to represent the variety of the company's users and to encourage inclusivity in media. The campaign features a series of films that highlight the most searched-for subjects of the year, and it is followed by a social media presence that invites people to contribute their tales and experiences.

These are just a few instances of effective inclusive media planning projects that have been implemented by corporations and groups in recent years. These initiatives demonstrate the importance of considering diversity, equity, and inclusion in media planning, and they highlight the impact that inclusive media planning can have in promoting positive representation of diverse communities and in fostering greater understanding and empathy among different groups.